ROBOTS

ROBOTS

by Robin Kerrod

Illustrated by
Tudor Art Studios

GRANADA

Published by Granada Publishing 1982
Reprinted 1983, 1984

Granada Publishing
8 Grafton Street, London W1X 3LA

British Library Cataloguing in Publication Data

Kerrod, Robin
Robots. – (Granada guide series; 22)
1. Automata – Juvenile literature
I. Title
629.8'92   TJ211

ISBN 0 246 11893 8

Printed and bound in Great Britain by
Collins, Glasgow

Contents

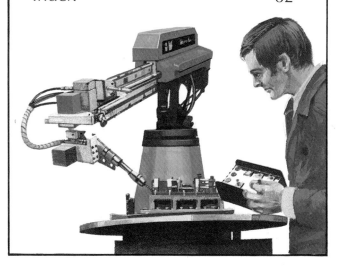

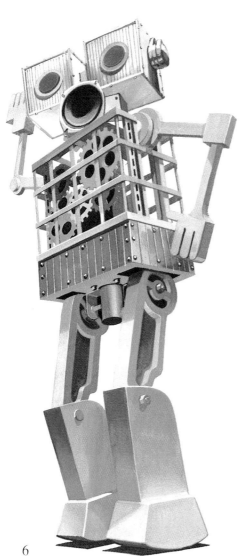

Robots at Large

Robots have been a favourite theme in science fiction for decades; now, thanks to spectacular advances in technology, particularly in the field of electronics, they are science fact. Already our wages may be calculated by robots. Our electricity and telephone bills are prepared by robots. Many of the cars we drive are put together by robots. Robots fly our aircraft for most of the time. And there are robots that can do housework, teach children and even play chess. These robots, however, seldom appear in human form as they do in fiction.

It is difficult to define precisely what a robot is. Generally speaking, it is a device or mechanism that can replace humans in certain situations. Its physical form is governed by the precise task it has to perform. To make a robot in human form – a mechanism called an android – is extraordinarily difficult and, for most purposes, unnecessary. The human body is a highly versatile mechanism capable of performing a great variety of tasks. A robot can perform particular tasks that are too tedious, time-consuming or dangerous for humans and so they are usually purpose-built.

It is in Japan that the impact of robots has been greatest. In Tokyo's Robot Pavilion 'happy' robots perform for onlookers (far left), trying to dispel the bad image robots have gained over the years. Practical robots, like this experimental guide dog (left), are less attractive but more useful.

Over to George . . . and Mildred?

George was one of the earliest robots to appear on the scene and after 70 years is still as popular as ever. George flies planes for most of the time. It is the automatic pilot, or autopilot, and was called George by human pilots happy to hand over a lot of tedious work to it. George was invented by the Sperry gyroscope company in 1913 and is built from gyroscopes. Once set spinning, gyroscopes remain pointing in the same direction. The human pilots hand over to George when the plane is on its correct course. By means of its gyroscopes, George can sense any vertical or horizontal change in direction and take corrective action.

Robot expert Professor Meredith Thring has remarked that more routine work is done by intelli-

Gyroscopes monitor any change in flight path as the aircraft shifts its axis, and George immediately moves the appropriate controls to bring the aircraft back on course.

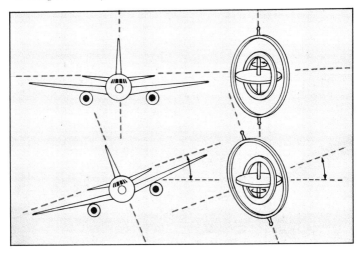

gent people in the home than anywhere else in modern civilization. So, in an age when robots are taking over repetitive and boring jobs in industry, what chance is there of them taking over in the home? The main problem is that housework is actually complicated to perform. It involves a great variety of different activities, that take place in different parts of the house. To make a domestic robot even half as versatile and mobile as a housewife would be exorbitantly expensive.

This is Reckett Industrial Division's answer to the housewife's plea for a home help. It can polish, sweep, dust and vacuum clean.

No papers litter this office desk which holds a complete information processor.

In the office, however, the robot excels. Here it takes the form of a computer terminal, which has such facilities as filing, stock control, calculating wages, word processing and printing. Filing is done electronically on magnetic tape or 'floppy discs', which cuts down on the amount of paperwork that needs to be done. Any filed item can be instantly recalled on a video display unit (VDU).

Robots are now being used in teaching medicine, in the form of life-size dummies, or body simulators. In most respects these act and respond identically to humans, but they can be programmed with various disorders and will afterwards give a computer print-out of any examination performed upon them. Silent Sam on the other hand works in the streets, warning of road works and flagging down the traffic.

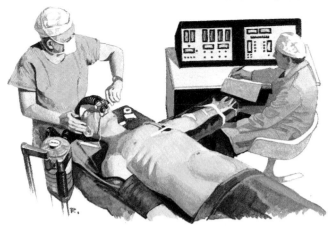

Life-size dummies, or body simulators, (above) behave like humans when medically examined.

Stanford University's 'complete' robot Shakey (below) is an advanced experimental robot.

Robot Silent Sam (below) can be seen on traffic control duty in Europe and the United States.

11

Rise of the Robots

Present-day robots have their roots in ingenious mechanical devices called automata that people contrived in ancient times. At Thebes in Egypt in about 1500 BC there was, it seems, a statue of King Memnon which gave forth beautiful sounds every morning.

In Greece in the 4th century BC, a mathematician named Archytas of Tarentum, inventor of the pulley and the screw, made a mechanical pigeon that could fly. A century later Ctesibius invented all manner of ingenious devices, including a water-operated organ and a clepsydra, or water clock. This was not the first clepsydra – the ancient Egyptians used them – but it was notable because it incorporated an automatic device that kept the water level constant. It worked

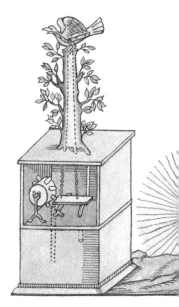

17th century illustrations of the singing statue of Memnon (below) and an ancient bird automaton, both activated by the Sun's rays.

The famous 'Peacock Fountain' was used for washing hands. When water entered the bowl, a figure emerged to offer soap, followed by another with a towel.

in much the same way as the float chamber in a modern car-engine carburettor.

Hero of Alexandria, who lived in about AD 150, was also a master inventor. His mechanical gadgets were driven by flowing water, falling weights and even steam. His aeolipile, forerunner of the steam turbine, is his best known work. But he also designed a slot machine for dispensing holy water; a bird that could, apparently, fly, drink and sing; an automatic theatre and a hydraulically operated statue of Hercules fighting a dragon. Hero described many of these devices in his book *Automatopoietica*.

In the Far East and Near East over the following centuries fascinating automata were made – in China, Japan, India and Arabia. The so-called Peacock Fountain depicted in a book about Arabian automata known as the 'Treatise of Al-Jazari', was an automatic soap and towel dispenser.

One of the finest automata of the 18th century was Pierre-Jacquet Droz's 'Young Writer', preserved in a Swiss museum. Its mechanism (below) is very complex.

In Europe in the Middle Ages the philosophers Albert Magnus and Roger Bacon took an active interest in automata and may have made them. The invention of the mechanical clock in the late 13th century provided a suitable mechanism for powering automata. Clock and automaton were combined in the 'jacquemart', or jack. The jacquemart consisted of one or more figures, powered by the clockwork mechanism, which struck bells in the clock tower to sound the time.

By the 18th century toymakers were turning out elaborate automata, often as human figures that could talk, play music, write and even play chess.

14

One of the most celebrated inventors of these toys was the Frenchman Jacques de Vaucanson.

Vaucanson also applied his inventive mind to more practical matters and outlined the workings of an automatic loom. This was later (1801) taken up by his fellow-countryman Joseph Marie Jacquard whose famous loom was controlled by a series of punched cards. Two other automatic devices came into use in the 18th century that used the principle of 'feedback', which is vital in automatic control systems. The two devices were the windmill fantail, which keeps a windmill's sails pointing into the wind, and the steam-engine governor, which keeps the engine running at constant speed.

Robots in Fiction

The term 'robot' first came into the language through the medium of fiction. It was coined by the Czech playwright Karel Čapek in the early 1900s, and came into more widespread use after the production of Čapek's play *Rossum's Universal Robots* in Prague in 1921. In this work robots are humanoids – human-like machines that can be factory-made quickly and cheaply. The word robot comes from the Czech word 'robota', meaning forced work, or slavery. So robots were conceived as slaves of the human race. They were artificial men, or androids.

It is not only in modern fiction that robots appear. Mary Shelley, second wife of the famous poet, wrote about the most famous artificial man in her horror story *Frankenstein* (1818). Frankenstein was a scien-

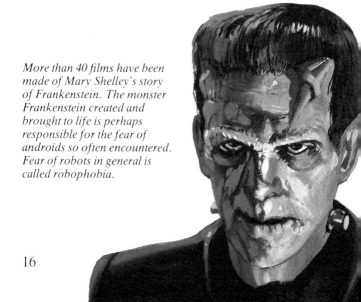

More than 40 films have been made of Mary Shelley's story of Frankenstein. The monster Frankenstein created and brought to life is perhaps responsible for the fear of androids so often encountered. Fear of robots in general is called robophobia.

tist who built a 'man' from parts of corpses and brought it to life. But it turned out to be a monster. Loathed and rejected, the monster rebelled against its creator and became an instrument of evil.

Mary Shelley subtitled her book *The Modern Prometheus*, harking back to a Greek myth that names Prometheus as the creator of man. Prometheus shaped man from clay and water, and the goddess Athene breathed life into him.

Maria (left) in the 1926 film Metropolis is perhaps the most beautiful robot creation. More functional in appearance, and nasty with it, is Gog (above) in a 1954 film of the same name.

Many other notable robots/androids have appeared in films and television over the years. Some are friendly and endearing creations, like Robby the Robot and the comedy duo of *Star Wars*, R2D2 and C3PO. Others, however, are cast in a malevolent mould, like Gog and the 'exterminating' Daleks from the Dr Who adventures.

If it came to a fight, R2D2 and C3PO (below) and Robbie the Robot (far right) would be no match for the sinister Dalek (centre) whose major aim seems to be to exterminate any being – or robot – that crosses its path.

These 'bad guys' have perhaps given robots a bad name, to such an extent that today people harbour grave doubts about the wisdom of introducing robots into our lives. They are frightened of the consequences of robots 'taking over'. To allay such fears, leading science-fiction writer Isaac Asimov suggests that robots should be programmed to obey three basic principles, which have become known as the laws of robotics: a robot (1) must not injure a human being or allow him to come to any harm; (2) must obey the orders of a human being, unless they oppose law 1; (3) must protect itself, unless this opposes the other two laws. What happens to robots that flout these laws can be seen in the film *2001*.

Anatomy of Robots

In the real world scientists emulate Prometheus to practical purpose. Their aim is to create robots that can carry out the same functions as humans so as to replace them in certain situations, particularly in industry. The new Prometheans do not seek to create robots in their own image because the human body is not necessarily the best design for every application.

But robots are composed of systems and sensors that parallel human nervous systems and sense organs, and often artificial limbs as well. And they have an electronic 'brain' – a computer. The development of the microprocessor, or 'computer on a chip', has meant that robots can now be equipped with a very powerful brain indeed, and can be programmed to do complicated tasks. In fact, development of the brain has really outstripped development of other robot systems. The brain is now capable of controlling much more complicated components than are currently available. Communicating with robots is also an awkward process which has to be done through a halting computer language, but direct voice control is not far away.

Robot scientists can learn much by studying the similarities between communications and control systems in human beings and in machines. This branch of science is known as cybernetics, a word coined by the American Norbert Wiener in 1948.

Robots are built with components and systems that perform similar functions to parts and systems of the human body – though they are of course not as complex or compact.

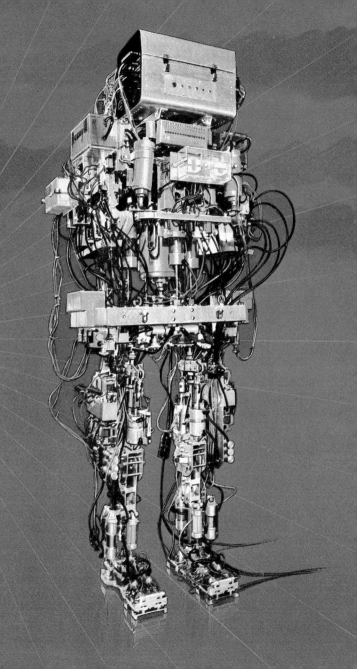

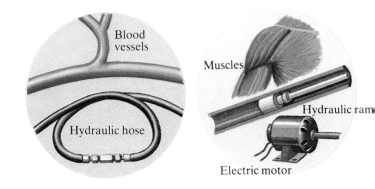

Blood vessels

Muscles

Hydraulic hose

Hydraulic ram

Electric motor

When making humanoid robots we can also learn from the field of bionics, or biological electronics. Bionic hands and arms are now available, for example, worked by the minute electrical impulses generated by body muscles. As well as 'non-working' replacement parts, such as plastic eyes and arteries, ceramic/metal hip joints and so on, researchers are continually creating new working parts, such as radioactive heart pacemakers to help keep the heart pumping. If the kidney and heart fail, they can at present be replaced with a transplant from a human donor. But maybe soon totally artificial hearts will become practicable.

By the end of the century it is thought that practically all the human organs could be replaceable. This could lead to a being who is part human, part machine, rather like the Bionic Man who featured in the popular television series *The Six Million Dollar Man*. He (or it) was rebuilt from the barely alive wreckage of an astronaut who crashed on returning to Earth. Another name for such a being is cyborg, a contraction of 'cybernetic organism'.

Robot Systems

The kinds of components and systems of which robots can be composed are easy to compare with parts and systems in the human body. A microphone converts sound waves into electrical impulses, while a loudspeaker does the reverse. They mimic the funcion of the human ear and voice. A photocell or TV camera converts patterns of light into electrical pulses, mimicking the eye.

The electrical signals from the microphone or camera are equivalent to the signals that flow through the human nervous system. In the robot

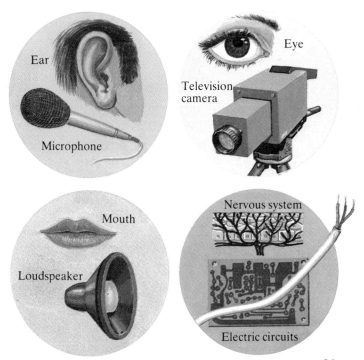

Ear

Microphone

Eye

Television camera

Mouth

Loudspeaker

Nervous system

Electric circuits

they are carried by copper wires or printed circuits. Instead of blood vessels, the robot has hydraulic piping containing hydraulic fluid. It flexes its muscles by means of electrical motors or hydraulic rams, worked by hydraulic pressure.

Communications and Control

As in the human body, communications and control systems in the robot can be very complex, which is one reason why their study became a separate science – cybernetics. The illustrations shown here demonstrate some of the major aspects of them – remote control, memory, sensors, automatic operation and feedback. Feedback is the vital element, allowing the possibility of self-control.

Aeromodellers use remote radio control to steer their planes.
Remote control is a feature of many robots.

Some of the latest push-button phones (right) are available with a limited memory to store often-repeated numbers. Robots require an extensive memory.

Guided missiles (right) have sensors that enable them to seek out their target. Robots require a range of sensors to seek information about their environment.

An automatic kettle (left) switches itself off when it has boiled. Robots require many automatic systems to function efficiently.

A room thermostat (right) switches itself on and off automatically, acting on information fed back by its sensor. Robots require feedback systems if they are to be self-controlling.

25

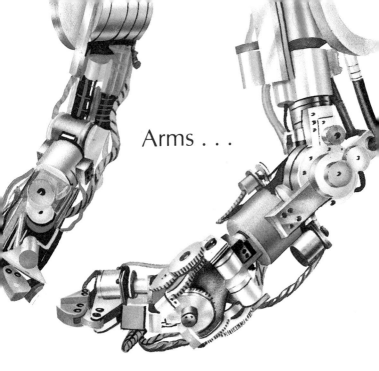

Arms . . .

Reproducing the human arm is not easy! The most complicated mechanism so far devised can perform only about 10 independent movements, as opposed to about 40 for the human arm. Some advanced robot arms have been built with flexible fingers containing sensors that give them a sense of touch. Others are being coupled to electronic eyes so that they can function more independently, like the human arm. The human arm is guided to its objective unconsciously by what the eyes see.

Making a robot mobile is most simply done by putting it on wheels. This is alright for travel over smooth ground but not much use for travel over rough ground. A tracked robot is better but can still be easily halted. Legs are really best, but imitating the human leg is even more difficult than imitating the arm. One of the major problems is balance. In this respect four legs are better than two.

Walking machines are not as novel as you might think. Some have been used in farming and excavation work for the past 40 years. One of the best known of the modern walkers is a four-legged truck. It was built by General Electric for the US Army. Its driver controls it by movements of his arms and legs, which are linked to the legs of the vehicle.

. . . and Legs

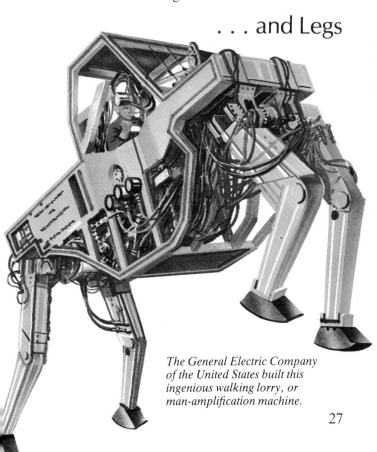

The General Electric Company of the United States built this ingenious walking lorry, or man-amplification machine.

27

The Brain

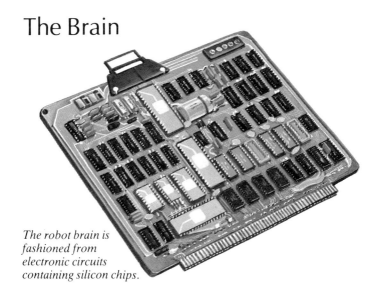

The robot brain is fashioned from electronic circuits containing silicon chips.

There was a time when the brain was the weak link in robot systems, but this is no longer true. An electronic brain can now be built about the same size as the human brain and with equivalent 'brainpower'. It is a series of silicon chips and other electronic components linked together on a printed circuit board.

The robot's brain is of course a computer. It is not like the human brain, capable of independent thought. It can only slavishly obey instructions given to it by a human being. But once equipped with these instructions and suitable data, it can perform superhuman feats. The same computer could theoretically be programmed to guide a space probe to Uranus, operate an oil refinery, sort out the wages of employees in a multinational company, and still find time to beat a Grand Master at chess! Although computers at present have no intelligence as we know it, it seems that they could acquire 'machine

28

intelligence', an artificial intelligence. Already some computers can learn from their experiences (a field of study known as heuristics). Others can teach themselves to solve problems rather than relying on instructions from humans. They seem to 'know' how they work better than the humans that created them do, and consequently make decisions better.

Hardware and Software

In computer terminology the physical components of a computer are called its hardware. The instructions and data fed into it are called its software. The hardware differs from computer to computer. Robot machines often contain only part of the computer system and are linked externally to the other parts.

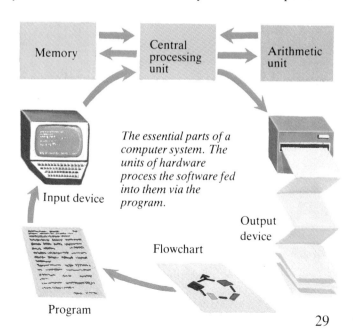

The essential parts of a computer system. The units of hardware process the software fed into them via the program.

```
IBM  IBM INFORMATION SERVICES LIMITED
                                          IBM COLUMN  11

TITLE  BILLING                                  PROJECT

1  BILLING: PROCEDURE OPTIONS (MAIN);
2    NEXTCARD: GET DATA (MORNO, OBAL, PAYM, RATE
3              CHARGE= OBAL*RATE/12;
4              PRINPAID = PAYM-CHARGE;
5              BALANCE = OBAL-PRINPAID;
6        PUT DATA (MORNO, OBAL, CHARGE, PR
```

Part of a programming sheet, showing the language used.

In a typical computer system, instructions are fed into the computer in the form of a program through an input device. This is often a keyboard with a video display unit (VDU). The central processing unit acts on the program and issues instructions to the arithmetic unit to process data from the memory. It then feeds the results to an output device, such as a printer. Or the results may be displayed on the VDU.

The data are handled by the computer in the form of numbers using the binary number system. This system uses only the digits 1 and 0, which can be represented in the computer's circuits by the flow or non-flow of an electric current.

The set of instructions fed to the computer is called the program. It also has to be converted into binary numbers. But this does not have to be done directly by the programmer. He writes the program in a simplified language, which the computer itself understands and converts into binary code. Three computer languages are widely used – Fortran, Cobol and Basic.

Before the programmer writes the program, he has to work out precisely what he wants the computer to do. He carries out what is called a systems analysis, which details the exact operations the computer must perform. He sets this out in the form of a flow chart that converts the operations into a sequence of Yes/No decisions, which can be coded 1/0 in the computer.

The Miracle Microchip

Today you can buy a computer no bigger than a typewriter which is more powerful than a room-sized computer of 20 years ago. What has caused the revolution is a wafer-thin sliver of silicon a few millimetres square, called the silicon chip. This chip

About 300 separate and identical chips are obtained from a single slice of silicon.

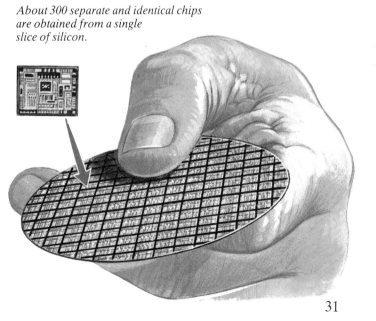

contains thousands of microscopic electronic components, such as transistors, resistors and capacitors, linked together to form complete electronic circuits. The components are not separately assembled, however. They are actually formed in position in the same piece of silicon crystal. They form what are called integrated circuits. The first integrated circuits were produced in the United States in 1958.

The chips used today contain tens of thousands of different components crammed into an area of about 30-40 square millimetres. They can hold as many as 64,000 bits, or units, of information. The most advanced chips can by themselves carry out most of the functions of a computer. They are called microprocessors. Equipped with microprocessors, all kinds of machines can be turned into robots.

Hundreds of identical chips are prepared at the same time on circular slices of pure silicon crystal. They are built up layer by layer by a lengthy series of photographic masking, doping and etching techniques. The masks are first made about 250 times life size and then reduced photographically.

Doping consists of treating unmasked areas of the chip with a vapour containing, for example, phosphorus. The phosphorus enters the silicon and forms a region that has different electronic properties from its surroundings and forms the basis of, say, a transistor. To build up the complete transistor, this process is repeated several times.

Finally a thin layer of aluminium is deposited and then masked and etched to make the necessary connections to an external circuit.

The 16-bit microprocessor chip (right) can carry out the control functions of a computer.

Robot Assistance

Hardiman

With due modesty, it can be said that we humans are versatile and inventive creatures, endowed with a well-developed brain. But we are comparatively weak, and we cannot tolerate conditions much different from those around us.

So we must use machines to extend our puny physique and help us withstand dangerous environments. The machines we use can be called robots because they do carry out human-like actions, even though they require the close involvement of a human to work. These are generally thought of as low-level robot devices, as opposed to the high-level robot devices now coming into use in industry, which require virtually no human involvement.

The exoskeleton is a powered external skeleton which can magnify the muscle power of a human being. Some exoskeletons have been developed to help physically handicapped people to walk. Others, such as the Hardiman, look forward to an industrial application in factories and on construction sites.

Exoskeleton suits will also find application in space when large space structures are built. The astronaut-manned manoeuvring unit tested by the American company Martin Marietta is a forerunner of this.

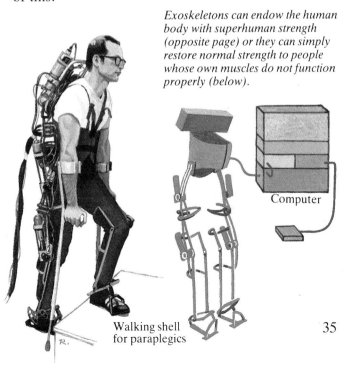

Exoskeletons can endow the human body with superhuman strength (opposite page) or they can simply restore normal strength to people whose own muscles do not function properly (below).

Computer

Walking shell
for paraplegics

Keeping a Safe Distance

One of the earliest applications for robot-assisted devices was in the atomic energy industry, where uranium is a major raw material. Uranium is very dangerous because it is radioactive – it gives off invisible and penetrating radiation that destroys the body cells. Even in relatively small doses it can be fatal. Extreme precautions must therefore be taken to protect personnel. Radioactive material is always stored and transported in containers lined with lead, and handled in protected enclosures by remote manipulators.

The human operators, safely outside, control the manipulator's arms with their own hands via a special hand grip. They see what they are doing through

Telechiric devices allow the handling of dangerous radioactive materials. They are sensitive enough to grasp flasks (below) and to remove fuel from the fuel elements of a nuclear reactor (opposite).

With robot assistance hot metal can be plucked from a furnace, at the behest of a worker seated comfortably far away.

leaded glass windows or mirrors. In more sophisticated robot manipulator systems, movement of the arms may be under computer control, and television cameras may be used to see what is happening.

Man-controlled robot devices can be designed to operate at a considerable distance, by sending the appropriate signals by wire or radio. These are sometimes call telechiric devices, the word telechiric meaning working from a distance.

Some robot experts believe that there is a bigger future for telechiric devices than for robots themselves, for such devices can be designed to combine the best features of man and robot. The pure robot can carry out a sequence of operations efficiently, but it cannot vary its method of working if operating conditions change, unless it is elaborately programmed. Though a human is in general a worse worker than a robot, he has the capacity to cope with changing situations and alter his pattern of working accordingly to achieve the desired goal. Put robot and human together, and you have a formidable combination.

Remote robot manipulators find plenty of application in hazardous operations in industry. In foundries, forging plants, press shops and heavy engineering works, they handle hot castings, and feed workpieces into dangerous machines while their human operator controls them from a safe distance. Soldiers and police often call on the service of robots in the fight against terrorist bombers. The bomb-disposal robot has a flexible arm on which is mounted a

The remote eyes of a robot probe search a vehicle for bombs. Sadly, no robot can match the skill of the brave bomb disposal men who may go into action if the robot's search is positive.

television camera which scans any object thought to contain a bomb. It is also used to place explosive charges to blow up any suspect bomb. Similar robots can be equipped with fire-fighting equipment and sent close to the heart of a fire, where human fire-fighters could not venture (see frontispiece).

Protection of a different kind is required for those who venture into the ocean deeps, prospecting for submarine deposits of oil and minerals. Special reinforced diving suits are used with power-assisted arms and articulated joints, so that divers can work under such crushing pressure. They often work in conjuction with deep-sea diving vehicles, equipped with a variety of manipulator arms, which can turn off valves, drill and weld.

A diver in a JIM diving suit works on the sea-bed with a submersible. He can call upon its extra muscle power when required.

Robots in Industry

The introduction of robots into industry is the latest event in a revolution that has been going on for nearly three centuries – the Industrial Revolution. This was sparked off by the invention of labour-saving machines, at first in textile manufacture, which were operated by the workers. Later came improved automatic machines, which performed a series of operations automatically and required the operator only to switch them on and off. Then in the 1950s machines came under computer control – they became automated.

Automated machines are robots. They not only automatically carry out a complex sequence of operations, but also keep a check on the product they turn out to ensure that it is exactly to specification. They are self-regulating – correcting themselves as they go along.

In their turn mechanization and automation have led to much greater productivity per worker and form the basis of the modern manufacturing method of mass production. Another essential feature of this method is the moving assembly line, on which relatively unskilled workers assemble in sequence identical parts turned out by precision machines.

In recent years robots have also been invading the assembly lines and seem set to take over most routine assembly tasks in the not-too-distant future.

Most large manufacturing companies are investing heavily in industrial robots to improve their produc-

Robot welders, looking like birds with beaks, 'attack' the cars as they pass by on the production line.

tive efficiency. In 1982 Japan had by far the largest population of advanced industrial robots – over 10,000. In Japan the human work-force work happily side by side with robots and give them pet names, usually of pop stars and baseball players. The United States had about 5000 advanced robots in 1982, West Germany 2500 and Britain about 1000.

Automated Machine Tools

In order that workers – or robots – can put together parts on an assembly line, these parts must be virtually identical and interchangeable.' To make them you need precision machine tools, which shape with great accuracy.

The modern precision tool is a robot. It performs all of its functions – picking up, positioning, cutting

Punched paper tape (above) produced by computer is used to control many automated machine tools.
Two modern technologies – robot control and lasers – are combined (right) to produce a versatile and precise profile-cutting machine.

44

with one tool, repositioning, cutting with another tool, and so on – automatically under computer guidance. The computer issues instructions by means of a punched-paper or magnetic tape, which carries a code in the form of numbers. This method of operation is called numerical control.

In some production processes a number of numerically controlled machine tools work in concert, each performing one sequence of operations on a workpiece before handing it on, via a so-called transfer machine, to another machine tool. This kind of operation happens, for example, in the manufacture of car engine blocks. As many as 30 machines working together carry out several hundred handling, positioning and machining operations that transform a rough casting into a finished engine block ready for the assembly line.

Pick-and-Place

The first of the modern generation of advanced industrial robots was put on the market by the American company Unimation in 1962. It was a relatively simple device designed to 'pick-and-place' – pick something up here and place it down there. It differed from a simple mechanical device because it could be programmed.

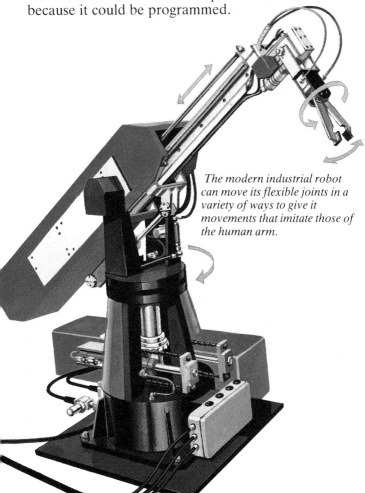

The modern industrial robot can move its flexible joints in a variety of ways to give it movements that imitate those of the human arm.

A robot is being taught to carry out its allotted task by a fellow worker.

Since the late 1970s more sophisticated robots have been introduced into industry and now perform complicated tasks that skilled workers once carried out. Their main use so far has been in the car industry for welding and paint spraying.

These robots look rather like ungainly giant birds, with long necks and beaks, which 'attack' car bodies as they pass by on the production line. Typical is Hall Automation's robot, which has a mechanical 'arm', jointed at an 'elbow', and also a 'wrist' and 'hand'. These 'limbs' and joints give it the same freedom of movement as the human arm and hand. In addition its arm can move in and out, which is something the human arm cannot do. The arm and joints may be worked electrically, hydraulically (by liquid pressure) or pneumatically (by air pressure).

Before the robot arm can perform its task, however, it must be taught what to do. A human operator programmes the robot by guiding its mechanical arm through the exact motions it has to perform. The robot memorizes the motions and thereafter can carry them out independently.

The impact of robots on industry is well illustrated by these pictures showing a conventional car factory (above) with a human work-force and one that has been automated by the use of robots (opposite).

Tireless Workers

Robots continue to improve by leaps and bounds. Unimation's latest PUMA robot and the Italian Sigma and Pragma robots can position their delicate 'fingers' to an accuracy of a fraction of a millimetre. They are thus suitable for simple assembly tasks, such as tightening nuts and screws.

The next generation of robots in industry will be much more flexible because they will be equipped with electronic eyes. They will not only be able to see objects but also recognize their shape. This means that the robots will be able to locate, pick up and position objects as well as carrying out work on them.

There are many advantages in employing robots in industry. They are tireless workers, able to work virtually non-stop for day after day with only an occasional break for servicing. During this time they perform with the same precision, suffering neither physical fatigue nor the boredom that afflicts human workers. Also, robots can work in unpleasant conditions where humans might complain of, for example, heat, smoke, glare and noise.

Because they can work virtually non-stop, robots soon repay their investment. And they are gradually coming down in price, whereas the wages of human workers are constantly rising. So robots both increase productivity and bring down production costs.

Robot miners are remote controlled from above ground and can work seams inacessible or dangerous to humans.

One of the biggest manufacturers of industrial robots is Fujitsu Fanuc of Japan, whose factory in the foothills of Mt Fuji turns out some 500 machine tools and 350 robots a month. It achieves this production target with a work-force of only 100 people and 30 robots. It has robots making robots. Without them it would require 500 people to maintain its production.

The mining industry is notoriously hazardous for its workers. Now a robot has been invented able to work in narrow and dangerous coal seams. It is equipped with microphone 'ears', television-camera 'eyes' and a gas-analyser 'nose'. It is guided by remote control by a human miner located safely at the surface.

Remote mining vehicles could also be the answer for dredging for mineral-rich manganese nodules or drilling for oil on the deep-ocean floor.

The oil industry at present boasts extensive robot involvement in the refining of crude oil into marketable products like petrol and kerosene. Despite its colossal size and complexity, an oil refinery is operated apparently by just a handful of people. But the real 'brains' behind it are the electronic brains of a powerful computer. The computer closes and opens valves, switches pumps and heaters on and off, and does a multitude of other things to keep the refinery running smoothly. No human could do so many necessary things at the same time, nor react so quickly when conditions change.

Robot scoops may be one method of harvesting precious manganese nodules from the ocean floor.

Robots in Space

In space there is no atmosphere to breathe. Temperatures in the sun are scorching hot and in the shade deathly cold. Deadly ultraviolet rays and atomic particles stream unceasingly from the Sun. It is thus exactly the kind of environment which it is sensible to send robots to explore instead of human beings.

Man's exploration of space really began on October 4, 1957, when the Russians launched the spacecraft Sputnik 1 into orbit a few hundred kilometres above the Earth. Sputnik 1 was the first artificial satellite of the Earth. It was simply a radio transmitter. The first American satellite, Explorer 1, was launched on January 31 the following year. It pioneered robot exploration of space by reporting conditions around it.

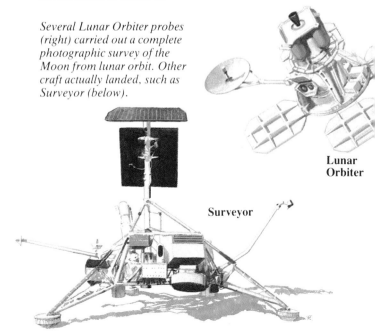

Several Lunar Orbiter probes (right) carried out a complete photographic survey of the Moon from lunar orbit. Other craft actually landed, such as Surveyor (below).

Lunar Orbiter

Surveyor

The most obvious target for robot exploration has always been the Moon. The first successful lunar probe was the Russian craft Luna 2. It crash-landed on the Moon in 1959, and in the same year Luna 3 sent back photographs of the far side of the Moon.

By the early 1960s the Americans had plans to send men to the Moon. But first they despatched robot probes, such as Lunar Orbiter and Surveyor, to photograph possible landing sites and test the nature of the surface. American lunar exploration culminated in the Apollo missions between 1969 and 1972, during which 12 astronauts explored the Moon on foot. The Russians, however, were content to send robot probes. Some landed on the Moon, scooped up samples of soil, and returned to Earth. Others took the form of a wheeled vehicle, equipped with television-camera eyes and other sensors. Called Lunokhod, they were guided remotely from Earth.

The first wheeled vehicle on the Moon was the Russian probe Lunokhod, which landed in 1970. During its 322-day life span it travelled more than 3 km.

Lunokhod

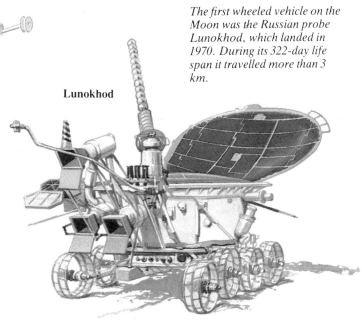

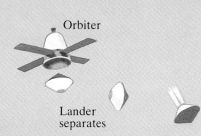

Orbiter

Lander
separates

*Viking spacecraft made the first
successful landings on Mars in
1976. The landers separated
from the orbiters, and used
parachutes and retrorockets to
achieve a soft landing.*

Parachute opens

Probing the Planets

The Apollo missions demonstrated that it is possible, though very expensive (25,000 million dollars), to send men to the Moon. It is at present impossible to send them to the planets. Even the nearest planet, Venus, never gets closer to the Earth than about 50 million kilometres. And we have as yet no technology to enable us to journey that far into space and return safely. So we send robots instead, equipped with television-camera eyes and all kinds of other instruments to probe alien worlds.

The Russians pioneered planetary exploration in 1961 when they sent a probe to Venus. And it is their Venus probes that have brought them most success. They have landed several Venera probes on the scorching (450°C) surface of the planet. In 1982 Venera 13 and 14 took pictures from the surface that showed Venus's sky to be a yellowish-orange colour.

The Americans have had even more spectacular success in robot planetary exploration, having by 1981 explored in detail all the planets out to Saturn. Their two Viking landing missions to Mars in 1976 followed on from several successful Mariner missions, which mapped the entire Martian surface. The Viking landers not only photographed the surface from close-up and reported on the weather, but also sampled the curious red soil and searched for organic matter, which might indicate the presence of life. But they searched in vain.

In 1973/4 the American Pioneer 10 and 11 space probes journeyed beyond Mars, across the rock-strewn asteroid belt, to the giant planet Jupiter. Pioneer 11 was then redirected to Saturn, which it reached in 1979.

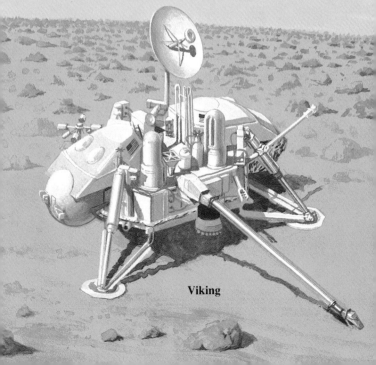

Viking

The Pioneer probes made many new discoveries about the two planets, recording powerful magnetic fields, picturing violent storms and finding many more moons. But they were outshone a few years later by the Voyager probes, which performed flawlessly and returned the most spectacular pictures of the planets and their moons. They snapped volcanoes erupting on Jupiter's moon Io and revealed that Saturn's beautiful ring system is actually made up of thousands of separate ringlets. They also discovered that Jupiter and Saturn have between them at least 37 moons, not 22 as was originally believed.

The Space Shuttle

Even when humans travel in space, the spacecraft are robot controlled. Powerful computers in the launch and mission-control centres and on board the spacecraft do virtually all the work. Manned spacecraft are so complex that only computers can handle the thousand-and-one operations that need to be carried out at the same time during the flight.

The computers on board the space shuttle, for example, carry out something like 300,000 operations per second at times of exceptional activity such as lift-off. The orbiter has in fact five on-board computers that directly or indirectly control the whole flight. It is thus very much a robot craft.

The first shuttle flight was long delayed because of problems with the orbiter's main engines and the tiles that form the craft's heat shield. But when the maiden flight of the shuttle system did take place, on April 12 1981, it was a spectacular success. The orbiter, named Columbia, spent 54 hours in space and glided to a pinpoint landing in the Mojave desert

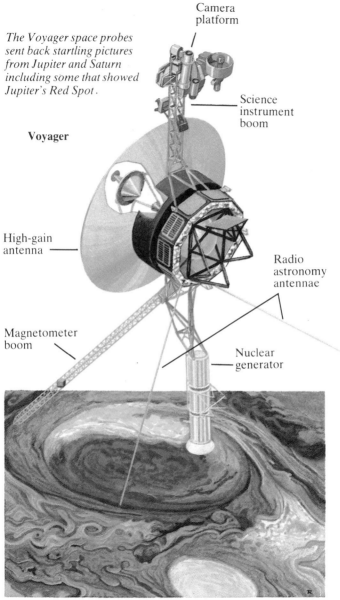

The Voyager space probes sent back startling pictures from Jupiter and Saturn including some that showed Jupiter's Red Spot.

Voyager

Camera platform

Science instrument boom

High-gain antenna

Radio astronomy antennae

Magnetometer boom

Nuclear generator

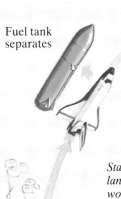

Fuel tank
separates

Orbiter enters
orbit

Orbiter launches
satellite

*Stages in the take-off and
landing procedures of the
world's first re-usable
spacecraft, the space shuttle. In
orbit (opposite) it launches
satellites by means of its remote
manipulator arm.*

Boosters
separate

Orbiter
re-enters
atmosphere

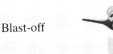

Blast-off

Orbiter glides
to a runway
touchdown

in California. Within a year it had twice returned to orbit, something that no craft had ever done before.

With the shuttle comes a new era in space activities, an era in which space launchings become routine. Columbia, and her sister craft Challenger, Discovery and Atlantis, are so revolutionary because they are designed to be re-usable. So are the booster rockets that fire on lift-off.

Because most of the shuttle system is re-usable, space flights are becoming less expensive. The orbiter can carry enormous amounts of cargo in its cavernous payload bay, which measures some 4.5 metres in diameter and 18 metres in length. It is thus able to carry several satellites into orbit at once.

One of the most important payloads the shuttle is designed to carry is Spacelab which has been built by the European Space Agency to fit into the orbiter's payload bay. It is a fully equipped scientific laboratory in which scientists and engineers can carry out a

variety of experiments in medicine, engineering, metallurgy, remote sensing, astronomy and many other branches of science.

In the near future fully equipped modules like Spacelab will be carried into orbit by the shuttle and assembled there into larger space stations. Some will serve as permanent space laboratories. Others will eventually serve as a base to build other space structures, including fully automated industrial complexes, and solar power plants which will beam energy down to Earth.

Robots to the Stars

Although we and our robots have taken a short step into space, some people foresee a time when we shall explore beyond the confines of our solar system, seeking other solar systems. Even the nearest stars, though, are over 40 million million kilometres away. It would take centuries to reach them with our present technology.

We shall of course send robots into the unknown first to blaze a trail for us. The British Interplanetary Society has already put forward a design for such a robot, called Daedalus. Powered by controlled thermonuclear fusion, it would aim for Barnard's star, which is thought to have a system of planets. After a 50-year flight, Daedalus would reach the system and acquire data about it, which it would then transmit back to Earth. If the reports are favourable, mankind and his robot friends might eventually embark on interstellar travel and colonization of alien worlds.

The starship Daedalus reaches another star system after a journey of nearly half a century.

Index

Credit: page 18, courtesy of Lucasfilm Ltd.
          page 19 (left), courtesy of the BBC Torrance Nation.